THE
TRUE BLUE
GUIDE TO
AUSTRALIAN
SLANG

THE TRUE BLUE GUIDE TO AUSTRALIAN SLANG

Edited by Jenny Hunter

NEW HOLLAND

First published in Australia in 2004 by
New Holland Publishers (Australia) Pty Ltd
Sydney · Auckland · London · Cape Town

14 Aquatic Drive Frenchs Forest NSW 2086 Australia
218 Lake Road Northcote Auckland New Zealand
86 Edgware Road London W2 2EA United Kingdom
80 McKenzie Street Cape Town 8001 South Africa

National Library of Australia Cataloguing-in-Publication Data:

The true blue guide to Australian slang.

ISBN 1 74110 192 1.

1. English language - Australia - Slang - Dictionaries.
I. Hunter, Jenny, 1955- .

427.994

Managing Editor: Monica Berton
Editor: Jenny Hunter
Project Editor: Liz Hardy
Designer: Karl Roper
Production Manager: Linda Bottari
Printed in Australia by McPherson's Printing Group, Maryborough

10 9 8 7 6 5 4 3 2 1

INTRODUCTION

Visitors to Australia often scratch their heads during an encounter with an Australian. Aussies are generally informal in both their behaviour and conversation, and the liberal use of slang is a feature of this informality.

Slang is the casual, spoken language of a country, which uses humour and metaphor. It is colourful and descriptive, and generally reflects the personality and history of a country.

Australian slang can be ironic and self-deprecating, but it can also be rude, crude, racist and cruel. I've included some 'offensive' examples but have tried to stay away from overt racism and relentless crudity. Some of the less polite words I've included reflect, I hope, the Australian personality.

Some crude slang is so colourful and amusing I had to include it. Two favourites in this vein are 'budgie smugglers' and 'dingo's breakfast'.

Australia's obsession with sport has added many great examples including the abuse 'white maggot' screamed at an Aussie Rules football umpire after an unfair decision.

You can see examples of some of the more entertaining Australian expressions in the feature boxes throughout the text. These boxes also demonstrate the regional variations in slang, such as the many different names that Australians have for a swimsuit.

Australia's white history, particularly early life on the farm and in the bush, has contributed some delightful phrases. I recently heard a football commentator saying about a coach and his team, 'Has he got the cattle?'. And there's 'Big hat, no cattle' a description of a farmer who has the hat but not much else. A recently published book was called *Ducks on the pond*, a shearing-shed phrase warning of the approach of women.

In the past, Australia's remoteness reduced the impact of external influences and, perhaps, this is one explanation for the development of a distinctive Aussie slang. The global village means we now have instant access to the rest of the world and vice versa. For better or worse, American culture dominates popular culture and influences our language. Let's hope the unique cultural mirror that slang gives us remains for future generations to enjoy.

ACKNOWLEDGMENTS

Researching this book has given me a great appreciation of Aussie slang. I've had assistance from a couple of people with a love of words. Simon Balderstone, who grew up on a farm and has a way with words, and John Bowan, a walking encyclopaedia, contributed significantly to the content of the book. Their humour and imagination is worth bottling.

The World Wide Web is a great source of information and misinformation. Thank goodness for GA Wilkes' *Dictionary of Australian Colloquialisms*, which has been on my desk for the duration.

Thanks to my Rogen International colleagues—your suggestions and enthusiasm for the project were a great starting point. And thanks to Fergie for staying out of my hair.

Jenny Hunter

A

A bit
An example of Aussie irony, when used at the end of a sentence. *Thorpey can swim a bit.*

A bit of a ...
Another example of Aussie irony. 'A bit of a loony' is a person who displays some loony qualities but is not a total loony.

Aerial ping-pong
Aussie Rules football, derogatively used by fans other other football codes.

Aggro
1. Visibly aggravated or very upset about something. *2.* Open confrontation, argument.

Agricultural shot
A wild hit at a cricket ball often over mid-wicket to 'cow corner'.

Akubra
An Australian-made farmer's hat.

All the go
Fashionable.

Also-ran
1. A nobody. 2. An unplaced horse in a race.

Amber fluid, amber nectar
Beer, a favourite Aussie drink.

Anzac
A member of the Australian and New Zealand Army Corps (ANZAC) who fought at Gallipoli in World War I. Anzac Day is celebrated on 25 April each year.

Argue the toss
Dispute a decision.

Argy bargy
A lot of talk, usually unnecessary, before a decision.

All prick and ribs like a drover's dog
Tall and skinny, but a goer. A throwback to the days when Australia rode on the sheep's back, and the drover and his dog were symbols of the nation.

Arsey
Lucky.

Arvo
Afternoon.

Aunty
Australian Broadcasting Corporation (ABC), the national public broadcaster.

Aussie
1. Australian (noun or adjective). 2. The Australian dollar.

Aussie Aussie Aussie, oi oi oi
Australian cheer, commonly heard at sporting events and made famous

during the Sydney 2000 Olympic Games. Still heard but now verges on being annoying and giving you the **tom tits**.

Aussie Rules
Australian Rules football.

Australian salute
Movement of the hand to brush flies away from your face.

Average
Bad. *This curry is a bit average.*

Awake-up to someone
Be aware of someone's tricks.

Ay, eh
A non-interrogative used at the end of a sentence by Queenslanders.

In more shit than a Werribee duck
To be in a great deal of trouble. Werribee, the Victorian town lying between Melbourne and Geelong, is not only the stamping ground of cricketer, Merv Hughes, but also the site of a well-known sewage farm.

B

B&S, bachelor and spinster ball
A formal dance held in a woolshed for young country people. Traditionally large amounts of alcohol are drunk and people sleep outdoors, wherever they drop. (Not to be confused with BS, which is shorthand for bullshit.)

Backblocks
The outer suburbs of a city.

Backchat
Reply to someone in an unnecessarily cheeky way.

Bad trot
A period when things are not going well in someone's life.

Bag someone
Criticise someone.

Baggy green
Australian Test cricket team cap.

Bail out
Leave a place, usually quickly.

Bail up
Have someone captive and **earbash** them.

Bald as a bandicoot
Very bald.

Balmain kiss
A headbutt, Aussie equivalent of the Liverpool kiss.

Bang on
That's right.

Bar flies
Pub regulars who spend quite a lot of time leaning on the bar **yarning**.

Barbecue stopper
A subject of conversation so compelling that Australians will interrupt a barbecue to discuss it.

Barbie, barby, BBQ
A barbecue, the only time most Australian men cook.

All over the place like a madwoman's breakfast
With this rather sexist image, Australian men conjure up a sense of total shambles. There are of course cruder alternatives to 'breakfast' in some variants of this saying.

Barmy army
English supporters of their sporting teams.

Barney
An argument, dispute.

Barrack
To cheer for your team.

Basket weaver
Someone from the 'soft' side of politics. They may be arty crafty types and advocate an alternative lifestyle.

Battleaxe
A cranky, nagging woman.

Battler
A working-class person struggling for a livelihood. During election campaigns, battlers are wooed for their votes. *Also* Aussie battler, little Aussie battler and, more recently, Howard's battlers.

Bean counter
An accountant.

Beanie
A knitted hat, sometimes with a pompom, which has occasional moments in the fashion sun.

Beanpole
A tall, thin person.

Bear pit
The Lower House in the NSW Parliament, where fierce political debate takes place. And where former Labor premier, Neville Wran, talked of applying a blowtorch to his opponents bellies.

Beaut, beauty
Exclamation of approval. *You little beauty!*

A DINGO DID IT
In the early 1980s, a baby disappeared from a tent near Uluru (then Ayers Rock). The mother was convicted of the crime but was later exonerated when further investigation revealed that a dingo probably took the baby. Hence a useful phrase where a dingo can be blamed for anything that goes wrong.

Beer belly, beer gut
A paunch associated with excessive beer drinking.

Beer o'clock
Time to finish work and have a beer.

Bee's dick
A very small amount or distance. *Thorpey beat Michael Phelps by a bee's dick.*

Bench warmer
A reserve in a sporting team who spends most of the games on the bench.

Berko
Someone who goes berserk or is angry in an unreasonable way. *Also* to go berko.

> **As busy as a one-legged bloke in an arse-kicking contest**
> *Overly pressured Australians are also said to be as busy as a one-armed bill poster in a high wind, or as busy as a one-armed milker on a dairy farm.*

Bickies or bikkies
Money, usually refers to someone who earns a lot of money.

Biff, biffo
Punch or punching, fighting, particularly during a football match.

Big ask
A request that may be hard to fulfil and might be an imposition.

Big Australian
BHP, now BHP Billiton, once the biggest company in Australia.

Big hat, no cattle
A person has the **Akubra** but has he got any livestock, i.e. looks the part but not the real thing. *Also* The smaller the property, the wider the brim.

Big note, big noter
1. To brag or boast. *2.* A person who brags or boasts.

Big smoke
The city (particularly used by country people).

Big spit
Vomit.

Billabong
A waterhole.

Billy, billy can
A tin container used to boil water over an open fire and make tea.

Billy cart
A child's unmotorised go-kart, usually homemade.

Bite
React to a provocative statement.

Bite your bum
An injunction to somebody to get lost.

Bitser, bitzer
A crossbred dog, a mongrel.

A LONG WAY AWAY
Back o' beyond
Back o' Bourke
Beyond the black stump
Bullamakanka
Outback
The back country
The mulga
The Never-Never
Woop Woop

Bloke
Australian male.

Blokette
A blokey woman.

Blokey
Overtly (and probably overly) masculine.

Bloody
The great Aussie adjective. A bloody good word, often used instead of very.

Blow
Mess (something) up. *She blew her exams because she didn't study.*

Blow-in
A stranger in town.

A head like a robber's dog
There is no adjective here, but, notwithstanding Australians' deep cultural sympathy with convicts and criminals (such as Ned Kelly), the implication is of considerable ugliness.

Blow that
Exclamation that you're not going to bother about something.

Blow through
Leave in a hurry.

Blow your dough
Spend all your money.

Blower
The telephone.

Blowie
1. A blowfly. 2. A person moving in, like a fly, to exploit a situation.

Bludge
1. Avoid doing your fair share. 2. Something which is easy to do.

Bludger
Someone who doesn't do their share, or doesn't do anything.

Blunnies
Leather workboots made by Blundstone.

Bob's your uncle
Everything's okay, problem solved, job done.

Bodgie
1. Shoddy, **shonky**, **dodgy**. 2. Mainly in the 1950s, an Australian 'teddy boy' with a distinctive hairstyle and way of dressing, who engaged in loutish, delinquent behaviour.

Bogan
1. A lout or hooligan (WA). 2. Someone unstylish (NSW).

Bogey, boogie, booger
Nasal mucus.

Boil the billy
Make a pot of tea, not necessarily with a **billy**.

AT THE PUB
Pony *A very small glass of beer (140ml)*
Middy *A 285ml glass of beer (NSW, WA)*
Pot *A 285ml glass of beer (VIC)*
Schooner, schooey *A 425ml glass of beer*
Stubbie *A 375ml bottle of beer*
Long neck, tallie *A 750ml bottle of beer*
Slab *A carton of two dozen cans of beer*
Two-pot screamer *Two drinks and you're drunk*
Your Wally (Grout) *Your* **shout**

Boilover
An unexpected result in a sporting event.

Bomb
1. An old car. *2.* A very high kick in rugby. *3.* A jump into water, tucked into a ball, with the aim of making a big splash. *4.* A large amount of money. *That must have cost a bomb!*

Bondi cigar
A piece of human excrement in the ocean. *Also* blind mullet.

Bonza, bonzer
Good, excellent.

Boofhead
A stupid person, often with an overly large head.

Bangs like a dunny door in a gale
This colourful expression may be heard among certain Australian sexist blokes, describing the sexual availability of girls of their acquaintance.

Boofy
Brawny but stupid.

Boogie board
A board for bodysurfing.

Boom-bah, fatty boom-bah
An overweight person.

Boomer
1. A kangaroo. *2.* A big surf wave. *3.* Excellent, first class. *4.* The name for the Australian national basketball team.

Boomerang
Something lent which the owner wants returned. *That book is a boomerang.*

Boots and all
Totally involved or committed.

Booze bus
Police van used for random breath testing of car drivers for alcohol.

Boring as batshit
Extremely boring.

Born in a tent
Describes someone who repeatedly fails to close a door. *Were you born in a tent?*

Bot
Borrow from others with little intention of repaying.

Bottler
Something outstanding, excellent (fit to be bottled).

Bottom of the harbour scheme
A tax evasion scheme. The term was commonly used in the 1980s

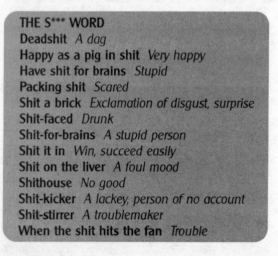

THE S*** WORD
Deadshit *A dag*
Happy as a pig in shit *Very happy*
Have shit for brains *Stupid*
Packing shit *Scared*
Shit a brick *Exclamation of disgust, surprise*
Shit-faced *Drunk*
Shit-for-brains *A stupid person*
Shit it in *Win, succeed easily*
Shit on the liver *A foul mood*
Shithouse *No good*
Shit-kicker *A lackey, person of no account*
Shit-stirrer *A troublemaker*
When the shit hits the fan *Trouble*

Bottoms up
A toast prior to drinking the whole glass of something all at once (usually beer).

Bounce the ball
A bounce of a ball by an umpire starts a game of **Aussie Rules**, hence, to start proceedings.

Bower bird
A person who collects useless objects.

Brass razoo
A worthless item.

Brekkie, brekky
Breakfast.

Brick
A good and reliable person. *You're a brick.*

Bring a plate
A request, usually to women, to bring some food to a function.

Bronzed Aussie
A description, frequently sarcastic, of the archetypal Australian male.

Buckley's, Buckley's chance, Buckley's and none
No chance, a forlorn hope.

Budgie
Budgerigar. A small parrot that lives in the wild in inland Australia but is popular as a pet. Not to be confused with the **singing budgie**.

You'll need to take a cut lunch
In a country of enormous distances (e.g. Sydney–Melbourne 900 kilometres, Brisbane–Cairns 1700 kilometres), this is a dryly humorous Australian way of saying that a long journey lies ahead.

Bugger me dead
Exclamation expressing deep shock or disappointment.

Built like a brick shit house
Someone of very sturdy build.

Bull, bulldust, bullshit
Expression of disbelief.

Bully for you
Sarcastic compliment.

Bum crack
Top of the buttocks exposed above pants, usually seen on workmen. *Also* builder's smile, coin slot, arse crack, brickie's cleavage.

AT THE GALLOPS
Horseracing is so central to Aussie culture that racing terms are frequently adapted to everyday life:
Correct weight *Official declaration of result*
Plunge *Rush of financial support for a project*
Ring-in *Substitute, imposter*
Roughie *Long shot, outside chance*
Urger *Self-serving tipster looking for his cut*

Bum floss
G-string (thong) underpants. *Also* anal floss.

Bum nuts
Hen's eggs.

Bumper
1. Cigarette butt. *2.* Short-pitched delivery in cricket.

Bundy on
To begin work, from Bundy clocks which were once used in the workplace to record the arrival and departure times of employees.

Bung
1. Put. *Bung it in the fridge.* 2. Not working. *The fridge has gone bung.*

Bung it on
Put on airs and graces. Used in a negative sense in the Australian practice of bringing down the **tall poppies**.

Bunny
Someone who accepts responsibility for a mistake, or has this responsibility thrust upon them.

Bunyip
An imaginary creature from the outback said to live around **billabongs.**

Bunyip aristocracy
1. Australians who **bung** on aristocratic airs and graces. 2. A derogatory description of an unsuccessful attempt to introduce a system of aristocracy in the mid 1800s.

Burnt offering
Over-cooked food, generally barbecued.

Bush capital
The nation's capital, Canberra.

Bush hanky
Blowing your nose by blocking one nostril with a finger and blowing the other nostril into the bush.

Bush lawyer
Someone with some knowledge of the law but no formal training, who relies on plausible but far-fetched arguments.

Your blood's worth bottling
An expression of warm, Australian appreciation for help given or a service rendered. See also **Bottler.**

Bush telegraph
Informal oral communication network, particularly involving rumour and gossip.

Bush telly
The stars in the night sky.

Bush tucker
Food made from native Australian plants; traditionally the food of Indigenous people but has made it into the **whitefella's** world.

Bushbash
Drive a vehicle off the road (or walk off the marked path) in the bush.

Bushie, bushwhacker
Someone who lives in the bush, usually a simple life.

Bushman's breakfast
No breakfast at all, just 'A piss and a good look round'. Compare to **dingo's breakfast**.

Bushman's clock
Kookaburra.

Bushwacked, bushwhacked
Exhausted, beaten, annoyed.

Buster
1. An accident or failure. To come a buster. *2.* Affectionate term for a male. *3.* A sudden, southerly squall in Sydney.

Busting
1. Badly needing to do something such as going to the toilet. *2.* Eagerness to do something. *He's busting to have a go.*

But
Used at the end of a sentence with the sense of 'however'.

C

Cab sav
Cabernet sauvignon wine.

Cackleberry
An egg. *Also* Cackle fruit.

Cactus
Useless, ruined. *I'm cactus after that big night out.*

Calendar coat
Jacket with two rear vents, i.e. lift the flap to see the **date.**

Call
A decision, for example by an umpire, which, depending on how it affects you, might be a bad call or a good call.

Call a spade a fucking shovel
Blunt and honest speaking, Australian style.

Cane
Beat someone in a game or competition.

Can't take his hand off it
A wanker, poseur.

Cark it, kark it
Die or break down.

Carn
Cry of encouragement, or barrack, for a sporting team. An Australian pronunciation of 'come on'. *Carn the Swans!*

Cashed-up
Have money in your pocket.

Catch you later
See you later.

Cellar dwellers
A sporting team at the bottom of the competition table.

> **BARKER'S EGGS**
> *An Englishman, Steve, spent his gap year in Australia and worked for a lawn-mowing company. On his first day, the boss took him to a house with very long grass. The boss' last comment before leaving Steve to it was, 'Watch out for the barker's eggs, mate'. Steve had no idea what he meant until the mower hit the dogshit.*

Chardonnay socialist
A new type of Labor Party supporter named after their predilection for chardonnay and their middle-class lifestyle. Viewed disparagingly by traditional working class members of the party. (And by conservatives, who, of course, only drink very expensive chardonnay.)

Chardy
Chardonnay.

Charge like a wounded bull (or buffalo)
Charge excessively high prices.

Chateau de cardboard
Cask (cardboard box) wine. *Also* Dapto briefcase and red handbag.

Cheap as chips
Very cheap.

Cheap drunk
Someone easily intoxicated.

Check you later
See you later.

Checkout chick
The person operating the cash register at a supermarket.

Chew 'n' spew, chew and spew
Fast-food cafe which sells food of dubious quality. Once referred to Chinese restaurants.

Chewie
Chewing gum.

Chewie on your boot
A football cheer intended to disconcert a player taking a kick.

Chief cook and bottle washer
A person who does nearly all tasks involved in a project or job.

Chigga
A person from the Hobart suburb of Chigwell viewed, unfairly, as uncultured.

Been in a good paddock
This disarmingly understated suggestion of obesity reminds us of the rural origins of the nation's wealth and the Aussie's love of horseracing.

Chip off the old block
Someone who shares characteristics of his or her parents.

Chock-a-block
1. Full, very crowded. 2. Caught in the act of sexual intercourse.

Chocker, chockers
Completely full of food or drink.

Choke one
Defecate.

Choof off
Leave.

> **BLUE or BLUEY**
> *A mistake or fight*
> *Blue heeler (police officer)*
> *Blue bottle (a danger in the ocean)*
> *Red-haired person*
> *Blue or red heeler (cattle dog)*
> *Summons for traffic offence*
> *Airline Virgin Blue used it ironically (blue meaning red)*
> *when they named their airline and painted the planes red.*

Chook
A domestic chicken. Includes chicken eaten as meat. *We have roast chook every Saturday night for tea.*

Chook raffle
A raffle often held in clubs and pubs with the prize being a frozen chicken.

Chuck a wobbly
Throw a tantrum.

Chuck in, chuck it in
Resign or give up.

Chucker
A cricket bowler who throws the ball instead of bowling it.

Chunder
Vomit.

Chunderous
Revolting, unpleasant.

Clacker
The bottom.

Claytons
A substitute for the real thing. From an ad for non-alcoholic drink made by Clayton's that was described as 'The drink you're having when you're not having a drink'.

Clock
Record the speed of something, e.g. speed camera, athlete.

Clucky
Feeling the desire to have a baby.

Clued-up
Well-informed.

Coathanger
Sydney Harbour Bridge.

Cobber
A mate, a friend.

Can talk under wet cement
*In a country which values the laconic, this Australian measure of garrulousness is one stage further up the scale than the ability to talk under water. See also **Earbash**.*

Cobber-dobber
One who informs on a **cobber**, and a very low form of life.

Cockie
A cockroach or a cockatoo.

Cocky, cow cocky
A farmer.

Cocky's joy
Golden syrup.

Coke-bottle glasses
Spectacles with thick lenses.

Coldie
A cold beer.

THE P*** WORD
A piss in the ocean *A small amount*
A pissant *A small, aggressive person*
Piss in someone's pocket *Behave obsequiously towards someone*
Piss into the wind *Futile action*
Pissed (as a fart, a newt, or a parrot) *Drunk*
Pissed off *Very unhappy or annoyed*
Piss-fart around *Waste time*
Pisspot *Someone who drinks too much*

Collywobbles
The nervous condition that adversely affects the Collingwood football team, and almost invariably at finals time. More generally, to be sick in the stomach.

Colourful racing identity
A person operating on the wrong side of the law, found at racetracks.

Come a cropper
Fall over, either literally or figuratively.

Come a gutsa, gutser
1. Fall over and hurt yourself. 2. Be part of a plan that doesn't work out.

Come again
Could you repeat that, please?

Come good
Succeed after prolonged difficulty.

Come in off the long run
Be aggressive.

Come off it mate
Be reasonable.

Compo
Worker's compensation. An important concept in Australian history and culture.

Comrade
Occasionally ironic term of affection between members of the Labor Party.

Conch, conchie, concho, conchy
Someone who is overly conscientious, a swat, or a conscientious objector to national service.

Cooee
Bush call or greeting to someone. Also a reference to the distance between people in the bush. *There are no pubs within cooee.*

Dressed up like a pox doctor's clerk
It is a bit hard to explain why this little known and uncommon employment group continues to be a byword for flashy over-dressing in Australia.

Cop shop
Police station.

Cop you later
See you later (said quickly, to get the full significance).

Corroboree
Aboriginal dance ceremony.

Cot case
Someone who is incapacitated, perhaps by overactivity.

UNIQUELY AUSSIE WORDS
Billabong *Waterhole*
Matilda *Swag*
Jumbuk *Sheep*
Swagman *Itinerant*

Coward's castle
Parliamentary chambers where things are said, without fear of legal action, which can't be said outside.

Cow-pat lotto
A game of chance in which a cow is placed in a paddock which has been divided into numbered squares. The winner is the person who bets on the square where the first cow-pat lands.

Crack the whip
Tell people to hurry up and get something done.

Cranky
In a bad mood.

Crawler
Someone who ingratiates themselves with their superiors. Nearly as bad (and just as common) as a **dobber.**

Crikey
An exclamation of surprise.

Crim
A criminal.

Croc
A crocodile.

Crock
A worn-out or injured old person (usually sporting).

Crocodile skin
Badly sun-damaged skin. *Also* lizard skin, handbag skin.

Crook
1. Sick, or something that is not functioning. *2.* A criminal.

Crook as Rookwood
Extremely sick. (Rookwood is the biggest cemetery in Sydney.)

Crooked on
Angry or annoyed at someone.

Cry ruth
Vomit.

Cunning as a shithouse rat
Very cunning.

Cup of tea, a Bex and a good lie down
Someone is overwrought and needs a rest.

I hope your chooks turn into emus and kick your dunny down
One of the nation's emblematic fauna combines with the ubiquitous dunny (toilet—traditionally of the outdoor variety) to form a typically colourful Aussie curse.

Cuppa chino
A cappuccino coffee.

Cut-lunch commando
A member of the Army Reserve.

D

Dack
Pull someone's trousers or pants down as a practical joke.

Dacks or daks
Trousers or shorts and sometimes underpants. (From a trademark.)

Dag
A lump of excrement-matted wool on a sheep's rear.

Dag, daggy
A nerd, someone who doesn't dress very smartly. Adjective describing that person.

Damper
Bread, made of flour and water, cooked in a campfire.

Date
Bottom, buttocks, anus.

Deadshit
A nerd, a turd, a goose, a jerk, an annoying person.

Deep north
Far north Queensland.

Deliver the goods
Produce what you've promised.

Demo
Abbreviation of demonstration, usually political.

Derro
A derelict or vagrant.

Digger
1. An Australian soldier. Originally a goldminer, then soldiers from World War I, but now refers to any soldier. 2. A general greeting, like **mate.**

Dingo's breakfast
A piss, a drink of water and a good look around.

COME IN SPINNER
Two-up is a game involving two coins being tossed into the air using a kip (small board). People in the ring bet on whether the coins will come down heads or tails. It's illegal to play two-up, but on **Anzac Day** *the police turn a blind eye.*
Fair go *Call prior to the coins being tossed*
Cockatoo *The lookout*
Floater *A coin which fails to spin when tossed*
Ringie *The person in charge of the school (game)*

Dinki-di, dinks, dinkum
True, genuine. A variation of fair dinkum.

Do a Melba
Make a comeback, return from retirement a number of times, as singer Dame Nellie Melba did.

Do bugger all
Do absolutely nothing.

Dodgy
1. Something suspicious or **iffy** is going on. 2. Something that is unsound or not of good quality. *His car looks a bit dodgy.*

Do your block, do your lolly
Get very angry, carry on angrily about something.

Dob
1. Inform on someone, to the police, management, teachers, etc. 2. Contribute money to a present fund.

Dobber
An informer or telltale. Historically, a reviled but only too familiar figure in Australia. A **cobber-dobber** is the most reviled species. Now undergoing an image change as a whistleblower.

Doco
A documentary.

Dog's breakfast
A shambles, a mess.

Dole bludger
Someone who receives the dole and is perceived as not making reasonable attempts to find employment.

Domestic
An argument with one's spouse.

Dry as a Pommy's towel
Very dry and thirsty indeed. Reflects the widespread Australian belief that bathing and showering are not widely performed in England. Hopefully, out of date. See also **Pongo.**

Done like a dinner
Comprehensively defeated.

Donkey vote
A vote cast without any thought or care about the outcome.

Don't give a rat's (arse)
Don't care.

Doodad, doover, dooverlackie
A device or gadget with a forgotten name.

Dorothy dixer
A question asked in parliament specifically to allow a propagandist reply by a minister. (After the agony aunt, Dorothy Dix.)

> **THE LUCKY COUNTRY**
> *'When I invented the phrase "The Lucky Country" it was quickly mis-understood as it quickly caught on … a phrase that was intended as an ironic rebuke became a phrase of self-congratulation.' Donald Horne, author of* The Lucky Country, *a term synonymous with Australia.*

Double Bay head-butt
The air-kiss greeting between people from Sydney's eastern suburbs.

Double-dipper
A person who has been both a state and federal **pollie** and who receives benefits from both generous superannuation schemes. More generally, a public servant who receives income from a public fund such as superannuation, as well as a salary from a subsequent public service position.

Double Pay
An alternative name for the posh Sydney suburb of Double Bay, based on the supposed prices charged there.

Down the gurgler, or plughole
Unsuccessful, wasted effort.

Down the track
At some point in the future.

Drag the chain
Slowing progress down.

Dreamtime
In Aboriginal mythology, the time in which the earth received its present form.

Drink with the flies
Drink alone.

Drongo
A stupid person.

Droopy drawers
A sluggish, apathetic person.

Drop your bundle
1. Lose control of the situation. *2.* Fail to deal with problems.

Drop your guts
Fart.

Dropsies
A bout of accidentally dropping things.

He's still got his lunch money from school
An Australian who is very careful with his money, if not actually a miser. Can be compared with a person who has short arms and long pockets.

Dry up
Be quiet.

Ducks on the pond
A warning to the men in a shearing shed that women are approaching.

Duckshove
Off-load your responsibilities to someone else.

Dud
1. Swindle someone. *2.* A thing or person that proves to be a failure. *3.* Duds, plural, refers to clothing.

Dumper
A wave in the surf which breaks violently, throwing swimmers into the sand, sometimes dangerously.

Dunlop overcoat
A condom. (Dunlop is a rubber manufacturer.) *Also* **franger**.

Dunny
Originally an outside privy, now any toilet.

Dunny budgie
Blowfly.

E

Earbash, earbasher
Harangue someone. One who harangues.

Easy wicket
A cosy job or position involving lots of money and little effort. (From cricket.)

Ekka
Brisbane Exhibition Grounds.

Emma chisit
How much is it? An interpretation of Australian pronunciation or **strine**.

Emu parade
A group of people picking up rubbish.

Esky
A portable icebox used for picnics.

Even blind Freddie could see that
Something very obvious.

CONFUSING BASTARD
G'day you old bastard. (Affectionate)
He's a mean bastard. (Descriptive and pejorative)
Poor bastard. (Sympathetic)
Pommy bastard. (Once critical, now usually affectionate)
Stupid bastard. (Factual)
You bastard. (Venomous, but can be grudgingly respectful)

F

Fair cop
1. A just sentence. *2.* An admission that you were caught out.

Fair crack of the whip
Be reasonable, don't go overboard.

Fair dinkum, fair dinks
True, genuine.

Fair enough
Okay, no problem.

Fair suck of the sav, fair suck of the sauce bottle
Give us a break

Fanny
Female genitals. (American use means bottom.)

Fart-arse around
Mucking about rather than getting on with something.

Fat cat
Someone who enjoys privileges because of their position or wealth.

Public servants are often disparagingly called this.

Feeding time at the zoo
A disorderly group of people jostling each other for drink and food.

Femocrat
A feminist bureaucrat.

Femonazi
A derogatory term to describe a woman who is seen as an extreme feminist.

Feral
1. Person who lives a life without mod cons, an extreme hippy. *2.* Very aggressive.

Fifth wheel
An extra or superfluous person or thing.

Filthy
Be annoyed with someone. *I'm filthy on you.*

Fit as a mallee bull
Very fit. *Also* Strong as a mallee bull.

Fix
Arrange matters close to the law or even illegally.

Fizzer
Something that wasn't up to expectations. (From an unexploded firework.)

Fizzle out
Fail after a promising start.

Don't come the raw prawn with me
The humble prawn has an honoured role in Australian cuisine and invective. This saying indicates a refusal by the speaker to be taken in by a hypocritical, self-righteous line of argument.

Flake
1. Shark used in fish and chips. 2. An eccentric person.

Flake out
Collapse from exhaustion, or another ailment.

Flaming
A euphemism for other swear words.

Flannie
A flannelette shirt.

Flash as a rat with a gold tooth
Someone who is ostentatious, overdressed and tasteless.

DON'T BUG ME
Overheard in a restaurant:
American tourist: How big are the insects on the menu?
Waiter: What insects?
American tourist: The Moreton Bay bugs.
Waiter: No, they're not insects.
American tourist: You call insects bugs in Australia, don't you?
Waiter: Yes, but these things are like big crabs.
American tourist: So they are much bigger than insects?
Waiter: Ahh, yes.

Flat as a tack
Very flat.

Flat chat
Very busy.

Floater
A piece of excrement that floats in the toilet bowl.

Flog
1. Steal something. 2. A person who is not up to the job.

Fluff
1. A fart. *2.* Fail to perform a task properly.

Foot in mouth disease
A propensity for saying embarrassing things.

Footie, footer, footy
1. Football, either rugby league or **Aussie Rules**. *2.* The football.

For openers, for starters
To begin with.

For the high jump
Facing punishment or dismissal from employment.

Foreman material
Dressed in working clothes smarter than usual.

Four-by-two
A piece of wood that measures four by two inches. *I hit him with a piece of four-by-two.* Usually pronounced 'Four b' two'.

Four-legged lottery
A horse race.

Franger
French letter, condom, **Dunlop overcoat, raincoat**.

Freebie
A service or item obtained free of charge. *See also* **lurk** and **rort**.

> **Flat out like a lizard drinking**
> *This picturesque reference to another important representative of Australia's fauna describes extraordinary hard work and non-stop activity.* See also **As flat as a tack.**

Fremantle doctor
A strong, cool, south-westerly wind which arrives in Perth and Fremantle in the afternoon.

Freo
Abbreviation of Fremantle, a port city south of Perth, Western Australia.

Fruitcake, fruitloop
A loony, someone slightly mad. *Nutty as a fruitcake.*

Fugly
Extremely unattractive, combination of 'fucking' and 'ugly'.

Full as a boot, a goog, a Catholic school
Drunk.

Full bore
Approach something with maximum enthusiasm.

Full of himself
Someone who has a very high opinion of himself.

Full of it
Talks a load of rubbish.

Full-on
Enthusiastically, energetically.

Funny farm
Psychiatric hospital.

Furphy
A rumour, a false story, misinformation.

Fuzzy-wuzzy angels
Papua New Guineans who helped Australian soldiers on the Kokoda Track during World War II.

G

G, the
Melbourne Cricket Ground or MCG.

Gabba
Brisbane Cricket Ground at Wollongabba.

Galah
A loud, rudely behaved person (from a noisy Australian bird).

Galoot
A foolish fellow.

Game as Phar Lap
As brave as Phar Lap, a legendary horse from the 1930s. *Also* A heart as big as Phar Lap.

Game, set and match
A convincing victory.

Garage door is open
A polite phrase used to tell someone their fly is undone.

Garbage guts
A person who eats a lot of any type of food.

Garbo, garbologist
Garbage collector.

G'day, gidday
Australian greeting. From 'good day'. *G'day, mate.*

Gee, gee whiz, geez
An exclamation of surprise.

> **FOR SEPTICS (YANKS)**
> **Biscuit** *Cookie*
> **Bonnet** *Hood*
> **Boot** *Trunk*
> **Bubbler** *Drinking fountain*
> **Chips** *Fries*
> **Entree** *Starter, first course*
> **Footpath** *Sidewalk*
> **G-string** *Thong*
> **Jumper** *Sweater*
> **Lift** *Elevator*
> **Nappy** *Diaper*
> **Petrol** *Gas*
> **Prawn** *Shrimp*

Gee up
To lift the spirits of someone.

Geezer
A look. *Give us a geezer at your new bike.*

Get a guernsey
1. Be chosen to do something. 2. Receive an invitation.

Get a handle on something
Understand something.

Get off at Redfern
Practice coitus interruptus in Sydney. (The last stop before Central Station.)

Get off at Richmond
Practice coitus interruptus in Melbourne. (The last stop before Flinders Street Station.)

Get on like a house on fire
Get on very well with someone.

Get stuck into
Attack someone verbally.

Get technical
Become pedantic and apply the strict rules.

Get the arse
Be dismissed from a job.

Get the nod
Approval to do or get something.

Get up your nose
Something is annoying you.

Get your arse into gear
Get organised so you can do something.

Greatest thing since sliced bread
Nowadays, many Australians, particularly in the inner suburbs of Australia's capital cities, would regard sliced bread as horrifyingly unsophisticated, but it retains its innovative place in popular parlance.

Ginormous
Incredibly huge, combination of 'gigantic' and 'enormous'.

Gismo, gizmo
A gadget.

Give it a burl, give it a whirl
Give something a try that you have not done before.

Give it a rap
Praise something.

Give it away
Give up on something or stop doing an activity. *She gave away netball after she hurt her knee.*

Give it the flick
Throw it away.

> **FOR TO AND FROMS**
> **Poms** *Aussie term of affection*
> **Pommy** *Aussie term of affection*
> **Whingeing Pom** *Less affectionate term*
> **Chips** *Crisps*
> **G-string** *Thong knickers*
> **Manchester** *Bed linen (not a football team)*
> **Soccer** *Football*
> **Truck** *Lorry*

Give me a bell
Ring me on the phone.

Give me the drum
Tell me what's going on.

Give someone a good rap
Praise someone.

Glad, gladdie
Gladioli, a flower made famous by Dame Edna Everage.

Go bush
Leave a city or town for a humble lifestyle in the bush.

Go for your life
An exclamation of encouragement to enjoy an activity to the max.

Go to billy-oh, go to buggery
Get lost, go away, leave me alone.

Go walkabout
From the Aboriginal practice of nomadic wandering in the bush. *1.* Lose concentration. *2.* Wander off.

Goat-faced
Drunk.

Good oil
The correct and hopefully profitable information.

Good on the fang
Have a good appetite.

Good sport
1. Someone who acts with grace in defeat. *2.* A willing female.

Goon
A flagon of wine.

Happy as a bastard on Father's Day
Here, the great Australian noun, 'bastard', is used, probably uniquely, in its literal sense. More typically, happy language is used ironically to convey misfortune.

Gosford skirt
A very short skirt, so called because it ends just below The Entrance. (The Entrance is a town north of Gosford on the NSW Central Coast.)

Got legs
Something has credibility and will keep going.

Grass castle
A large ostentatious house, built from ill-gotten gains, usually drug money.

Great White Shark
Nickname for golfer Greg Norman. Also, incidentally, a species of shark.

Grey nomads
Retirees who tour Australia in four-wheel drive vehicles, towing caravans.

Grey nurse
A $100 note. Also, incidentally, a species of shark.

Grudge match
A sporting match between traditional rivals.

Grumblebum
A person who habitually complains.

Gunner
Someone who promises a lot, but delivers nothing. *I'm gunner do this and I'm gunner do that.*

Gutless wonder
A cowardly person.

Gyp
Swindle or cheat someone.

H

Hairy eyeball
A disdainful or angry look.

Hammie
The hamstring muscle. Usually in a sporting context. *He's done a hammie and won't be able to play for the next three weeks.*

Handbag
An attractive male who accompanies a more successful woman, as an accessory, to social functions. (Not to be confused with a **manbag**.)

Handball
Adeptly pass a job to someone else, so they can't avoid saying yes.

Handbrake
A girlfriend who is sometimes viewed as an obstacle to male enjoyment with the mates.

Hang on a tick
Wait a short moment.

Happy as Larry
Extremely happy.

Happy little vegemite
Happy, contented Australian. (Vegemite is a traditional Australian yeast extract, to spread on bread.)

Hard yakka
Hard work.

Has he got the cattle?
Has a coach got the players to be able to win the game?

Have a go, you mug
Exhortation to someone to try harder; or to a batsman to show some aggression.

Have a lash
Take part in something.

> **IN TROUBLE**
> **Up shit creek** *In trouble*
> **Up shit creek without a paddle** *In serious trouble*
> **Up shit creek without a paddle in a barbed wire canoe** *In very serious trouble*

Have a squiz
Have a look at something.

Have an optic
Have a **perv**. Rhyming slang for optic nerve.

Have the wood on someone
Have an advantage over someone.

Have tickets on yourself
An inflated view of yourself.

Hayburner
A racehorse. Refers to cost of keeping them versus the amount they win.

Heart-starter
An alcoholic drink taken early in the day.

Heifer paddock
A girl's school.

Hens' night, hens' party
A girls' night out.

Hip-pocket nerve
The sensitivity of voters to money matters during an election.

Hit and giggle
Tennis or cricket played for fun rather than competition.

Hit the anchors
Put the brakes on.

Hit the jackpot
Achieve great success in an endeavour.

Hollow legs
Able to eat or drink a lot and not put on weight.

Home and hosed
About to cross the finish line in a race, usually in first place.

Hooley-dooley
An exclamation of surprise, amazement.

Handy as a screen door on a submarine
Useful as a glass door on a dunny
To these examples of Australian uselessness, one could add 'As useful as an ashtray on a motorbike' and 'As useful! as a hip pocket on a sock'.

Hoon
1. A show-off with little to back it up, and who displays anti-social behaviour. *2.* A fast, reckless driver of a car or boat.

Hop into
Criticise, attack someone.

Horizontal dancing, horizontal folk-dancing
Sexual intercourse.

Horse's doovers
Humorous translation of hors d'oeuvre.

Hostie
A flight attendant, from their previous job title 'air hostess'. *See also* **trolley dolly**.

Hot to trot
Eager and ready to do something.

Howzat
An appeal in cricket when the bowler asks the umpire if the batsman is out.

Humpy
A basic bush dwelling.

I

Iceberg, Bondi iceberg
A regular winter swimmer.

Iffy
Something risky, suspect or **dodgy.**

In good nick
In good condition, in good form.

In like Flynn
Well placed for success, e.g. in employment or sexually. After the Australian actor, Errol Flynn.

In the bag
Something is assured. *The game is in the bag.*

In the chair
It's your **shout**, your turn to pay for the drinks.

In your face
Someone or something very confronting, provocative or pushy.

Ins and outs of a cat's arse
An indication of the complexity and intricacy of an issue, from the colourful repertoire of former Prime Minister Paul Keating.

Irish curtains
Cobwebs.

Iron out
Fix some problems.

Iron someone out
Punch someone and knock them down.

It's a goer
The plan has been agreed to and will go ahead.

NICKNAMES
Bazza *Barry*
Dazza *Darrell*
Gazza *Garry*
Hazza *Harry*
Jezza *Jeremy, Alex Jesaulenko, former Australian Rules football great*
Kezza *Kerry*
Lozza *Larry, Laurie*
Mazza *Marion*
Shazza *Sharon*
Wazza *Warrick, Warren*

J

Jack
Nothing. *He doesn't know Jack.* *Also* Jack shit.

Jack of
To be jack of is to be fed up or have had enough of something.

Jackaroo, jillaroo
Trainee male or female worker on a cattle station or farm.

Jacky Howe
A navy singlet originally worn by shearers or labourers. (As worn by the champion shearer of the same name who set a record by shearing 419 sheep in a day using manual shears.)

Joe Bloggs, Joe Blow
The average man in the street. Person used as an example of an ordinary Aussie.

Joey
A baby kangaroo.

Jumbuck
Sheep.

Just down the road
A direction which may mean 100 metres or 1000 kilometres, or just around the corner.

London to a brick on.
In a land of keen punters, this expression describes the ultimately desirable outcome—a dead-set certainty. From horse racing originally but of general application.

K

Kafuffle, kerfuffle
A commotion.

Kangaroo-hop
Release the clutch of a car too quickly so that the car moves forward in a series of jerks.

Keg party
A party at which one or more kegs of beer are provided.

Keg-on-legs
1. A person who drinks an inordinate amount of beer. *2.* A short, obese person.

Kick
Wallet. *Nothing in the kick.*

Kick in
Contribute to a collection for a gift.

Kick on
Continue with an activity, e.g. a party.

Kick-to-kick
People kicking a football to each other.

Knock, knocker
1. Criticise. *2.* A critic.

Knockabout
1. Someone who has lived a rough and difficult life. *2.* Adjective describing someone with a very casual manner.

Knock back
1. Consume quickly, often in relation to beer. *2.* A refusal or rejection (including sexual).

Knock it off
An order to put an end to an argument or fight.

> **SPEEDOS—THE GREAT AUSSIE COSSIE**
> *Ball huggers*
> *Blue pointers*
> *Budgie smugglers*
> *Cluster busters*
> *Cock jocks, CJs*
> *Dick pointers*
> *Dick pokers, DPs*
> *Dick stickers*
> *Dick togs*
> *Racers*
> *Racing bathers*
> *Scungies*
> *Sluggos*

Knock off
1. A fake. *2.* To steal. *3.* To finish an activity, especially work.

Knock-off time
Time to finish work.

Knock on the head
Put an end to something.

Knockover
A pushover.

Knock yourself out
1. Expend a lot of energy doing something. *2.* An instruction to go right ahead and try something.

Knuckle
Used in relation to fist-fighting. *Go the knuckle. Fond of the knuckle.*

I could eat a horse and chase the jockey
I could eat a horse between two mattresses
These two expressions serve to remind us of the Aussie's love of a good feed and of the national addiction to horse racing and gambling generally.

L

Lagger
A police informer. *Also* **dobber**.

Lair
A brash, vulgar young man. *Also* mug lair, two-bob lair, lairise.

Land of the long weekend
Australia. (Compare New Zealand, Land of the Long White Cloud.)

Larrikin
A wild-spirited person who has little regard for authority. Often used to describe the Australian characteristic of irreverence.

Layabout
Someone who is allergic to work. *Also* **bludger**.

Lay-down misère
A certainty.

Leaks like a sieve
Someone who can't keep a secret.

Left for dead
Someone who is left behind, abandoned.

Left right out
A non-existent position on a sporting field i.e. a person has not been chosen to play in a team.

Leg opener
An alcoholic drink offered during the seduction of a woman.

Legless
So drunk that your legs no longer carry you steadily.

Leg-over
Sexual intercourse.

POINT PERCY
Drain the dragon
Have a leak
Have a slash
Johnny Bliss
See a man about a dog
Siphon the python
Shake hands with the wife's best friend
Shake hands with the unemployed
Splash the boots
Water the horse

Lemon
A machine that is faulty, broken or useless. Often used in reference to cars.

Let 'er rip
A phrase used to start a task, or some machinery.

Lezzo
Lesbian.

Lib
A member or supporter of the Liberal Party, which is conservative rather than liberal.

Lie doggo
Conceal yourself.

Lift your game
Smarten up, improve your performance.

Like billy-oh
1. Exclamation of enthusiasm. *2.* Fast pace.

Lippie
Lipstick.

Little boys
Cocktail frankfurts. *Also* cheerios.

Little Johnny
Prime Minister John Howard.

Long streak of pelican shit
Very tall, thin person.

Long as a wet weekend
A very long time.

Long paddock
The public areas along the edge of country roads which are used for grazing during droughts.

If it was raining palaces, I'd be hit by the dunny door
An Australian expression for chronic bad luck, illuminated by a characteristic Australian reference to the good old dunny.

Lurk
1. A dubious scheme or project. *2.* To furtively hang around. *3.* A cushy number. *Also* lurks and **perks**.

M

Mad as a cut snake
Crazy.

Mahogany row
A corridor of well-appointed offices for executives.

Manbag
A man's accessory which serves the same purpose as a woman's handbag, i.e. a useful way to carry bits and pieces. Recently popularised by that vision in vinyl, Kel, in the ABC television program, *Kath & Kim*.

Manchester
Household linen.

Mangle
Destroy or ruin.

Map of Tassie, Tasmania
Pubic area of a woman.

Mark
A catch in **Aussie Rules**.

Mate
A widely used form of address for men. Often used instead of a name, or if someone has forgotten your name.

Mean
To be good or accomplished at something. *He's a mean tennis player.*

Missus
Wife.

Mob
1. A mob of sheep. *2.* A gathering of people. *3.* Politician-speak for the electorate.

Mollydooker
A left hander.

> **THE TOP END**
> *The hot climate of the Northern Territory is thought to be the reason for the reputation of its people as casually dressed heavy-drinkers.*
> **Red centre** *Alice Springs and Uluru symbolise the mystical (but not geographic) centre of Australia.*
> **Darwin rig** *Dress for men for formal occasion (long trousers, shirt and tie). Also Territory rig.*
> **Darwin stubby** *A 2.25-litre bottle of beer.*
> **Shirt-and-sock occasion** *Dress code for a formal occasion.*
> **Territory confetti** *Ring-pulls from beer cans.*

Mondayitis
A lack of desire to work on Mondays.

Mongrel
A dreadful person or a very difficult job. Also, in a positive sense, fighting spirit. *He's got a bit of mongrel about him. Also* **Show some mongrel**.

Monkey suit
A dinner suit. *Also* **penguin suit**.

Monty
A certainty, particularly in relation to betting.

Moolah's in the cooler
The money is in the bank.

More front than Myers
Someone who is very pushy or audacious, Myer being a large, department store chain.

Motza, motser
A large amount of money.

Mushroom
A person who is deliberately kept uninformed. (Like a mushroom—they're kept in the dark and fed on bullshit.)

Mystery bag
A sausage. It's a mystery because it's unclear what's in it.

Myxo
Myxomatosis. A highly infectious viral disease introduced into Australia in a failed attempt to rid Australia of rabbits (which were also introduced from the **Old Dart**).

N

Nail
1. Perform a task correctly. *2.* Punish someone for a bad deed.

Nail-biter
An exciting game with a close finish.

Nasho
National service, conscription. A person who is conscripted.

Nats
Members of the National Party.

Nick off
1. Leave, disappear. *2.* A command to someone to disappear.

Nipper
A junior lifesaver.

Nitty-gritty
The most important aspect of something. *Let's get down to the nitty-gritty.*

No beg-pardons
No pleasantries, especially between traditional rivals in a grudge match.

No Captain Cook
Someone who doesn't pay debts on time, i.e. not an early settler. *He's no Captain Cook.*

No drama
No problems, happy to do that.

No flies on you
You're clever.

No worries
No problem, happy to do that.

No wucking furries, no wuckins
No fucking worries. *Also* no River Murrays.

Nobble
Interfere with a racehorse, e.g. by doping.

No-hoper
Someone who is hopeless.

> **I didn't come down in the last shower**
> *An assertion that the speaker is no mug. (In some parts of Australia, the drought can be so pronounced that people can't remember when the last shower was.)*

Nong
A fool.

Non-starter
Something which will probably not take place because it has little chance of success.

Norks
Women's breasts.

Norm
An average **bloke,** probably a couch potato.

Not a bad sort
An attractive woman.

Not a brass razoo
Totally broke. *I don't have a brass razoo.*

Not bad
Good. Most often used when asked how you are.

Not happy Jan
A phrase which became popular following its use in a television ad. More recently, it has been adapted to *Not happy John* as a book title referring to the Australian Prime Minister, John Howard.

Not much chop
Not very good.

Not the full quid
Not very intelligent.

Not within a bull's roar
Nowhere near (a measure of distance).

Nothing to write home about
Unremarkable.

THIRSTY
As dry as a Pommy's towel.
As dry as a dead dingo's donger.
Man is not a camel.
Lubricate the larynx.

O

Ocker, ockerdom
A person displaying the qualities of the archetypal Australian working **bloke.**

Ockerina
The **ocker's** female counterpart.

Off the beaten track
Not the usual way to go, the scenic route.

Off-load
Pass something undesirable onto someone else.

Off-sider
Assistant.

Oi or oy
An exclamation calling for attention.

Old Dart
Britain, especially England.

Oldies
Parents. *Also* olds.

On a good wicket
From cricket. *1.* On to a good thing, possibly a well-paid job with not much work. *2.* Living well.

On his hammer
In close pursuit of someone.

On spec
Sight unseen.

On the blink
Not working, particularly machinery.

On the boil
A game or situation is heating up, becoming interesting.

> **Like a rat up a drainpipe**
> *To take agile advantage of a situation, especially sexual. In Australia, the rat's image is no better than elsewhere.* See also **Cunning as a shithouse rat** *and* **Flash as a rat with a gold tooth**.

On the knocker
That's precisely right.

On the Murray (cod)
On credit. Rhyming slang for the nod.

On the nose
Something or someone that is unsatisfactory, i.e. smelly or suspect.

On the outer
Excluded or ostracised.

On the rantan
Having a big night out.

On the turps
Heavy drinking.

On the wallaby track
Go from place to place in search of work.

Once over
A quick examination of something.

Oncer
A flash in the pan, something that happens only once.

One for Ron
Saving it for later (derived from later on).

One-armed bandit
Old-style poker machine.

One-handed salute
A wave to keep the flies away. An **Australian salute**.

POLLIE SPEAK #1
Former Prime Minister, Paul Keating, is a master of colourful phrases, some of which came back to bite him.
'The recession we had to have.'
'This is the budget that brings home the bacon.'
'Downhill, one ski, no poles' on his leadership style.
'Throw the switch to vaudeville' when questioned on his ability to make the transition from treasurer to prime minister.
'I'm in the grenade throwing business. Occasionally, I drop one beside my foot, but I get many direct hits.'
'I've been watching you, and you're a low flyer.'

Onya, onya mate
Well done. From 'Good on you mate'.

Open slather
A free-for-all, everyone can have a go.

Out like a light
1. Go to sleep as soon as your head hits the pillow. 2. Unconscious after a punch.

Outlaws
Humorous variation of in-laws.

Owner operator
A euphemism for wanker.

Lower than a snake's belly
Lower than a snake's duodenum
The more elegant of these variants was used by Tammie Fraser, wife of former Australian Prime Minister Malcolm Fraser, to describe what she saw as scurrilous criticism by her husband's political opponents.

P

Pack it in
Give up on something.

Pack your kit
Pack up all your possessions and go.

Packer whackers
Defibrillators in all NSW ambulances. (Installed following the near-death experience of Australian media tycoon, Kerry Packer).

Packing death
Scared.

Pakapoo ticket
Untidy, disordered.

Passed the use-by-date
The usefulness of something or someone has passed.

Pav
A pavlova, a meringue dessert with cream and fruit filling.

Penguin suit
A dinner suit. *Also* **monkey suit**.

Perk
1. Vomit. *2.* Fringe benefit.

Perv
Act as a voyeur, particularly in relation to the opposite sex and often at the beach.

Pick a fight
Provoke a fight.

Pick someone's brains
Ask an expert lots of questions to find out more about their subject.

POLLIE SPEAK #2
Former Prime Minister, Sir Robert Menzies, aka 'Pig Iron Bob', on his feelings for Queen Elizabeth II. 'I did but see her passing by, yet I love her till I die.'

Pick the eyes out of
Choose the best parts and leave the rest for others.

Pie floater
A meat pie floating in thick pea soup, originally a specialty from Adelaide.

Pigs bum, pig's arse
Rubbish! An exclamation of disbelief.

Piker
Someone who backs out of an arrangement or runs away from an argument.

Pimple on the arse of progress
Someone who holds back an enterprise, a naysayer.

Pinged
Caught doing something illegal.

Pinko
Someone who is thought to have communist or socialist beliefs.

Pitt Street farmer
A wealthy city person with minor farming interests. *Also* Collins Street farmer, Queen Street farmer.

PJs
Pyjamas.

Play possum
Hide from others and be very quiet, play dead.

Please explain
The response of former right-wing politician, Pauline Hanson, to a journalist's question on whether she was xenophobic.

Pocket boxer
A male who frequently has his hands in his pockets in order to fiddle with his genitals.

Pokie, pokies
Poker machine/s. Found in most Australian pubs and clubs.

Pollie
A politician. A job usually held in low esteem in Australia.

Pongo
An Englishman, possibly derived from 'As dry as a Pommy's towel'.

On for young and old
General mayhem, brawling, pandemonium. Originally a physical brawl at a sporting event on the field or in the crowd but can refer to any widespread dispute in politics, business, etc.

Prickle farmer
A city slicker who moves to a small farm but knows so little that he tends the prickles.

Prop
Stop suddenly.

Proppie
Not fully fit, **a bit** injured, e.g. a footballer with a bad **hammie**.

Proverbial
Used as a substitute for a rude word, i.e. 'In the proverbial' means in the shit.

Psych yourself up
Prepare yourself mentally for something.

Pub crawl
Going from pub to pub, hopefully not on all fours.

Pull the pin, pull up stumps
Leave, get out.

Pull your head in
Mind your own business.

Pull your socks up
An instruction from someone to smarten up, or improve.

> **TIGHT**
> *Death adder in his pocket.*
> *Mousetrap in his pocket.*
> *Scorpion in his pocket.*
> *Short arms, long pockets.*
> *Tight as a fish's arse.*
> *Wouldn't **shout** if a shark bit him.*

Put in
Make a good effort.

Put in the hard yards
Work hard and, therefore, deserve a good outcome.

Put someone in
Inform. *I've put you in with the coppers. Also **dob**.

Put the acid on
Apply pressure to test someone's resolve or commitment.

Put the billy on
Boil the billy, or kettle, to make a cup of tea.

Put the bite on, put the fangs into, put the nips into
Attempt to borrow money, often with coercion.

Open slather
An Australianism to describe any situation that is wide open and where you can do what you like, without hindrance or regulation.

Put the frighteners on someone
Scare someone.

Put the mozz on someone
Jinx someone.

Put up or shut up
An aggressive request to do something or be quiet.

Pyjama game
One-day cricket in which the players wear baggy, brightly coloured uniforms resembling pyjamas.

Q

Quack
Doctor.

Quacker
A Kawasaki motorbike.

Quandong
A person who lives by their wits.

Quiche-eater
A sensitive new age guy (SNAG).

Quoit
The anus, buttocks, arse. *Also* **date**, ring or freckle.

> **Off like a bucket of prawns in the sun**
> *This expression conveys a great sense of speed off the mark, much in the same way as that great (but sadly departed) Aussie icon, 'Off like a Bondi tram'.*

R

RM Williams
A manufacturer of country-style clothing, symbolised by its elastic-sided dress boots (Sunday best) and moleskin trousers.

Rabbit killer
A quick chop to the nape of the neck with the side of a hand.

Rabbit on
Talk a lot of nonsense.

Race off
Seduce someone (carries a suggestion of impropriety, possibly after recourse to **leg openers**).

Racehorse
A thin roll-your-own cigarette.

Rack off, rack off hairy legs
Go away.

Rafferty's rules
No rules.

Rag
A newspaper (used scornfully).

Rager
A person who parties long and hard.

Rah rah
Rugby union supporter. (Not to be confused with **RARA**.)

Railway tracks
Dental braces.

Raincoat
A condom, **Dunlop overcoat**, **franger**.

Rainmaker
A very high kick, with a football.

POLLIE SPEAK #3
National treasure and former Prime Minister, Gough Whitlam, has inspired Aussies over the years and some of his words have become part of the lexicon.
'It's time.'
'Maintain your rage.'
'Men and women of Australia.' (orig. John Curtin)
'Tiberius with a telephone.'
'Well may you say God save the Queen, because nothing will save the Governor-General.'

RARA
Rural and regional Australia. A term bandied about by politicians, marketers and other bullshit artists.

Rashie
A lycra swimming top worn to prevent sunburn and skin rashes.

Rat coffin
A meat pie.

Rat cunning
Shrewdness, slyness.

Rat on a string
A very small dog, e.g. a chihuahua.

Rat on stilts
A greyhound.

Rat power
Sarcastic description of a bowler's speed, i.e. half-rat power.

Ratbag
An eccentric or foolish person.

Ratshit
Broken, useless. *Also* RS.

Rattle your dags
Hurry up.

Rattler, red rattler
A train. Red rattlers are older suburban Melbourne trains.

Razor gang
A government budget committee which reviews all expenditure with the aim of cutting back wherever possible.

Razz
Tease.

Not worth a cracker
Yet another Australian measure of worthlessness. Not to have a cracker can be used in the same way as not to have a **brass razoo.**

Razza
Returned Services League (RSL) club.

Redback
A $20 note.

Red-hot
1. A favourite. *2.* Blatantly improper behaviour. *That's absolutely red-hot!*

Reg Grundies
Undies. *Also* reggies, reginalds, grundies.

Rego
Car registration.

Rellies, rellos, rels
Your relatives.

> **USELESS #1**
> *A brick short of a load.*
> *A banger short of a barbie.*
> *A couple of tinnies short of a slab.*
> *Couldn't train a choko vine to grow up a dunny wall.*
> *Couldn't find a grand piano in a one-roomed house.*
> *Couldn't organise a root in a brothel.*

Rent-a-crowd
A reference to people thought to attend demonstrations and public events at the drop of a hat.

Reps
In parliament, the House of Representatives.

Revolving door
High turnover, especially staff, coaches, chief executives.

Ridgy-didge
Authentic, all right, is that right. *See also* **fair dinkum, dinki-di.**

Right as rain
Everything is okay.

Righto mate, righto son
Okay.

Ringer
A fast shearer of sheep.

Ring-in
A substitute for the real thing, often used in horseracing.

Ripper
Something fabulous. *You little ripper! Also* ripper Rita.

Ripsnorter
An extraordinary person or thing.

Rissole
A Returned Services League (RSL) club.

Road train
Multi-trailered livestock truck usually only seen in the outback.

Roadie
A final drink for the road.

Rollie or roly
A roll-your-own cigarette.

Take your bat and ball and go home
To put on a tantrum, behave self-indulgently or make an exhibition of yourself, when not getting your own way. See also **Sook.**

Roll-up
The number of people who attend an event.

Romp it in
Win something very easily.

Root
Have sexual intercourse.

Rooted
Very tired.

Ropeable
Angry. Australian version of 'fit to be tied'. *Mum was ropeable when I told her I crashed the car.*

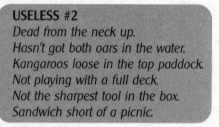

USELESS #2
Dead from the neck up.
Hasn't got both oars in the water.
Kangaroos loose in the top paddock.
Not playing with a full deck.
Not the sharpest tool in the box.
Sandwich short of a picnic.

Rort
1. A **lurk** or **perk,** often used in relation to the abuse of benefits available only to those at the top of an organisation. *2.* An unfair advantage to one group.

Rotgut
Very cheap alcohol.

Rotten
Extremely drunk.

Rotten egg gas
Hydrogen sulphide.

Rottie
A rottweiler dog.

Rough as bags, as guts
1. A description of a foul-mouthed person. 2. Loose morals. *She's rough as bags.*

Rough diamond
A person without refinement of manner but having an essentially good or likeable personality.

Rough end of the pineapple
A bad deal, or poor treatment.

Rounds of the kitchen
A verbal attack, or chastisement, on the home front by the **missus**.

Rub it in
Remind someone repeatedly of something negative.

Rub-a-dub-dub, rubbity
Rhyming slang for a pub.

Rubber johnny
Condom. *Also* **Dunlop overcoat, franger**.

Rubbery
Flexible or dubious, particularly in relation to statistics.

Rude finger
The middle finger. (Considered a rude signal when raised by itself.)

Promised the world and delivered an atlas
A good example of the Australian's contempt for his big-talking, under-achieving fellow citizen. See also **gunner** and **big hat, no cattle**.

Rugged
Involving hardship, unfairness or unpleasantness. *That's a bit rugged.*

Rugger-bugger
A rugby union player or supporter.

Run a book
Operate as a bookmaker informally or, more generally, bet on events not necessarily related to the racetrack.

Run like a hairy goat
A racehorse that doesn't perform as well as it could.

Run out of legs
Exhausted, used in sporting sense.

Run-in
A disagreement.

Runs on the board
From cricket, someone who is qualified to do something or has a record of achievement.

S

Sallies, Salvos
Salvation Army.

Salt mine
The workplace.

Saltie
A saltwater crocodile.

Sambo, sanger
A sandwich.

Sandshoe crusher
Cricket ball aimed at the feet of the person batting, invented by fast bowler Jeff Thomson.

Sav
A type of frankfurt sausage (saveloy). A battered sav on a stick, or Dagwood dog, is still popular at Australian fairgrounds.

Scab
A strikebreaker. (Historically very unpopular, like a **dobber** or a **crawler).**

Scads
A lot. *He's got scads of money.*

Scalper
Someone who buys tickets for an event, often sporting, then sells them outside the venue for a profit.

SCG
Sydney Cricket Ground.

Schmick
Very smart, stylish.

Schoolie's week, schoolies
The week after students finish high school and go to a place in the sun to celebrate.

> **USELESS #3**
> *The light's on but there's no-one home.*
> *The lift doesn't go to the top floor.*
> *Tim Tam short of a packet.*
> *Wouldn't know if you were up him with an armful of chairs.*
> *Wouldn't piss on him if he was on fire.*
> *Wouldn't work in an iron lung.*

Scone
1. The head. *2.* To hit someone on the head.

Scratchie
An instant lottery ticket.

Screamer
A spectacular mark in **Aussie Rules**.

Serve
A tongue-lashing. *I gave him a serve when he came home **goat-faced** at 4 am.*

Servo
A service (petrol) station.

Shack
A simply-built holiday house or hut in the bush.

Shagger's back
Back pain, humorously attributed to the strain of sexual intercourse.

Shark bait
Someone who swims further out than other swimmers or surfers.

Sheila
A girl or woman. *Also* sort, bird.

She'll be apples, she'll be jake, she'll be right
Everything will be okay.

Shellacking
A comprehensive defeat.

Shickered
Drunk.

Shift your carcass
Get going, move (usually from a seat).

Shiralee
A **swag**.

Shirty
Upset or angry. *No need to get shirty.*

Pull out, digger, the dogs are pissing on your swag
Invoking two quintessential elements of the Australian legend, former Foreign Minister Gareth Evans is said to have thus suggested to then Prime Minister Bob Hawke in 1991 that his time was up.

Shocker
1. A bad performance, usually sporting. *He's putting in a shocker.* 2. A bad person.

Shocks, shockers
Shock absorbers.

Shonk, shonky
A dishonest person.

Shooftee, shufti
A look, an inspection.

Shoo-in
A certainty to win something.

Shoot through, shoot through like a Bondi tram
Leave in a hurry. (Sadly, the last tram for Bondi left some forty years ago.)

RHYMING SLANG #1
Bag o' (fruit) *Business suit*
Barry (Crocker) *Shocker*
Billies, billy lids *Kids*
Bo-peep *Peep*
Captain Cook *Look*
China (plate) *Mate*
Goanna *Piano*
Gregory (Peck) *Cheque*
Stuart (Diver) *Survivor*

Shout
A round of drinks bought at the pub. *It's your shout.*

Shove off
Go away (said in a angry way).

Show pony
A person with more presentation than substance. *Also* **big hat, no cattle**.

Show some mongrel
Display courage.

Show you the ropes
Show you how to do a job.

Shrapnel
Small change, usually coins.

Silly season
Christmas holidays, when media outlets, because of the lack of hard news, run silly stories.

Silver bodgie, silver budgie
Former Prime Minister, Bob Hawke.

Silvertail
A member of the upper classes.

Simmer
Interjection requesting someone to calm down.

Sin-bin
Time-out place for footballers who have broken a rule of the game.

Singing budgie
Singer, Kylie Minogue.

Rather pick up a death adder than a shovel
A further example of the imaginative abuse to which the work-shy are subject in Australia. Also Wouldn't work in an iron lung and **Bludger**.

Sink the slipper
1. Kick someone in a fight. *2.* Metaphorically hurt someone when they're down.

Sit on a beer
Take a long time to drink a beer or decline the next round of drinks. *I'll sit on this one thanks, mate.*

Sitter
Something which should have been easily accomplished but wasn't. *He's dropped a sitter.*

Six o'clock swill
A hectic session of buying drinks when pubs closed at 6 pm.

RHYMING SLANG #2
Doh ray me *Dough (cash, money)*
Drop kick *Drop kick and punt*
Dad 'n' Dave *Shave*
Dead horse *Tomato sauce (particularly on a meat pie)*
Dog 'n' bone *Telephone*
Ducks and drakes *Hangover-induced shakes*
Jack 'n' Jill *The bill*
Jiminies (crickets) *Tickets*
Unlucky fried kitten *Kentucky Fried Chicken*

Skid-lid
A helmet worn by a cyclist.

Skinful
Too much alcohol.

Skite
1. To brag about personal accomplishments. *2.* Someone who brags about personal accomplishments.

Sky a ball
Hit the ball into the air.

Slave-labour
Hard work that is badly paid.

Slug
A financial impost usually inflicted on **Aussie battlers** by a heartless government.

Smoko
Tea-break at work, a great Aussie tradition.

Snaffle
1. Take something before others have a chance. *2.* Steal.

Snag
Sausage.

Snake's piss
Cheap, bad alcohol.

Snakey
Someone is upset or angry.

Soft-cock
A man perceived not to have the courage to do something, or stand up for what he believes in.

Soft touch
1. A person who is generous with time or money, and will lend or give it if asked. *2.* Someone who is a pushover.

So far up him/her, you can only see the heels.
A typically extravagant Australian version of the universally familiar idea of the arse as the focus of obsequiousness. Being 'up' oneself or somebody else is an important concept in this country.

Sook
A cry-baby, whinger.

Spanner in the works
A difficulty or obstacle in a process or project.

Spanner water
Extremely cold water (so called because it tightens the nuts).

Spare tyre
A roll of fat around a person's midriff.

Sparrow's, sparrow fart
Very early morning.

> **RHYMING SLANG #3**
> **Molly (the monk)** *Drunk*
> **Optic (nerve)** *Perve*
> **Oxford scholar** *Dollar*
> **On yer pat (malone)** *Alone*
> **Persian rugs** *Drugs*
> **Porkie (pork pie)** *Lie*
> **Rubbity dub** *Pub*
> **Septic (tanks)** *Yanks*
> **To and from** *Pom*

Spear off
Leave.

Speccy
Spectacular, particularly sporting achievement, such as a speccy mark in **Aussie Rules**.

Spill the beans
Divulge something that was being kept secret.

Spit chips
Angry. *She was spitting chips after I told her I'd lost the money.*

Spit the dummy
Someone who has had enough and throws a tantrum. *Also* a dummy spit.

Spook
A spy, an intelligence officer.

Spray
Criticise someone verbally; give them a tongue-lashing.

Spruiker
Someone who persuasively tries to convince others to buy or do something, a salesperson.

Sprung
Caught doing something improper or illegal, busted.

Square up
Settle a debt.

Squattocracy
The early landed gentry in the white settlement of Australia.

Squib
1. Behave in a cowardly way and chicken out of something. 2. A mean or paltry person.

Rare as rocking horse shit
Scarce as hen's teeth
There are many unique animals found in Australia—kangaroo, koala and platypus, to name some of the best known—but the rocking horse is, apparently, not one of them.

Squirrel grip
An illegal tackle in which pressure is applied to the testicles of the tackled player.

Squiz
A quick look. *Take a squiz at this.*

Stack
An accident, usually involving a motor vehicle.

Stand out like dog's balls
Extremely obvious.

Standover merchant
A bully or intimidating person.

'STATE' OF EXCITEMENT

Mainland, mainlanders *What Tasmanians call the rest of Australia and the people who live there*

Sin city *What Melburnians call Sydney*

Bleak city *What Sydneysiders call Melbourne*

T'other side *referring to Western Australia*

NSW *Cockroaches*

QLD *Bananabenders, cane toads*

SA *Croweaters*

TAS *Taswegians*

VIC *Mexicans*

WA *Gropers, sandgropers*

Stat dec
A statutory declaration.

Sticky, stickybeak
1. A prying, meddling, inquisitive person. *2.* Have a curious look or investigate something. *I'm going to have a bit of a stickybeak at the house for sale down the street.*

Stink
A fight during a football match.

Stinker
A very hot and humid day.

Stirrer
A person who sets out to deliberately cause trouble.

Stone the crows
An exclamation of surprise.

Stonkered
Defeated, exhausted.

Stony-broke
Totally without money.

Stoush
A brawl, often verbal.

Straddle the barbed wire fence
Two bob each way.

Streaker
A person who runs naked in a public place, usually at a sporting event.

Streaker's defence
It seemed like a good idea at the time.

Strewth, struth
An exclamation of surprise.

> **Stir the possum**
> *To disturb a metaphorical sleeping dog, to revive a dormant issue, to provoke an argument. Similar to 'stirring', generally, something done by a* **stirrer** *or sometimes a 'shit stirrer'.*

Strides
Trousers.

Strike a blow
Start or resume work.

Strike a light, strike me lucky
An exclamation of delight, pleasant surprise.

Strine
The distinctive pronunciation of the Australian language. *See* **emma chisit**.

Stroppy
Belligerent or angry.

Stubbies
A pair of men's work shorts (no longer fashionable).

SWIMMING COSTUME
Bathers *SA, TAS, VIC, WA*
Togs *QLD, SA, TAS, VIC, WA*
Cossie *NSW*
Swimmers *NSW*

Stubby
A small bottle of beer.

Stubby cooler, stubby holder
An insulator to keep a stubby cold.

Stuff
Ruin something. *I've stuffed my back.*

Stuffed
Exhausted.

Stuff-up
A failure which has arisen from a foolish or thoughtless error.

Stunned mullet
Dazed and unaware. *He sat there like a stunned mullet.*

Suicide blonde
A woman who has dyed her own hair blonde at home.

Suits
Professional men (and now frequently women), usually CBD-based.

Sunnies
Sunglasses.

Surf 'n' turf
A meal that has both meat and fish, usually in large quantities.

Suss
Something suspicious or suspect.

Suss out
Investigate or search something out.

Swag
A canvas bag or cover in which you keep your clothes and bedroll.

Swear like a trooper
Swear a lot.

Sweetener
A financial incentive.

The smaller the property, the wider the brim
This ironic expression takes the lash to those Australians who seek to convey a false impression of the breadth of their acreage. See also **Pitt Street farmer**.

Swifty
An act of trickery.

Swipe
Steal.

Switcheroo
A change.

Sydney or the bush
All or nothing.

THE F*** WORD
Fairy floss
Fark
Far out
Fruit tingles
Fudge
Flogging
Flipping
Freaking
Fricking
Frigging
Fugging

T

Ta
Thank you, thanks.

Tacker
A young child.

Taddie
A tadpole.

Take a pew
Sit down.

Take a shine to
Like someone, usually soon after meeting them.

Take a sickie
Take a day off work, perhaps without being sick.

Take someone to the cleaners
Take money from someone, clean them out of money.

Talk you blind
A pub bore who gives you an **earbashing**.

Tall poppy syndrome
The propensity of Australians to **bag** almost anyone who makes it to the top.

Tanked
Drunk.

Tantie
A temper tantrum.

Tassie
The island state of Tasmania.

Tea
Dinner, evening meal.

Technicolour yawn
Vomit.

> **INITIALS #1**
> BGO *Blinding glimpse of the obvious*
> BYO *Bring your own*
> BYOG *Bring your own grog*
> CRAFT's disease *Can't remember a fucking thing*
> D&M *Deep and meaningful (conversation)*
> DCM *Don't come Monday, i.e. you're sacked*
> DDH *Drop-dead honey*
> DFE *Dead fucking easy*

Tee-up
Make the arrangements for something.

Terrorists
Tourists.

Tetchy
Irritable, touchy.

Thick as two short planks
Not very bright.

Things are crook in Tallarook
The situation is no good.

Thingummyjig, thingo, thingie
1. A device or gadget with a forgotten name. 2. Something you can't describe properly.

Thongs
Sandals made from rubber.

Thugby
Rugby league football.

Thumbs down, thumbs up
Disapproval and approval.

Thunder thighs
A person with large thighs.

Thunderbox
An outside toilet.

Tick up
Obtain credit or build debt.

Ticker
Heart. Recently used in politics to describe whether leaders have courage, determination and commitment. *Has he got ticker?*

Thinks the sun shines out of his arse
A good illustration of the Australian attitude towards the person who is 'up himself'. In a nation of sun-worshippers, everybody knows one place where the sun never shines.

Tickets on yourself
A person who has tickets on him- or herself, is stuck up, or thinks they are cleverer than they actually are.

Tickle the ivories
Play the piano.

Tide's out
A glass or cup of something which isn't as full as you'd like it to be.

Timothy
A brothel.

Tin-arsed
Lucky.

Tinnie, tinny
1. A can of beer. 2. A light, aluminium boat.

> **INITIALS #2**
> FIGJAM *Fuck I'm good, just ask me*
> LCD *Lowest common denominator*
> LOMBARD *Lots of money but a real dickhead*
> OPs *Other people's cigarettes*
> POQ *Piss off quick*
> RS *Ratshit*
> POET'S day *Piss off early tomorrow's Saturday*
> TGIF *Thank god it's Friday*

Tip a bucket on someone
Heavily criticise someone.

Tired and emotional
A euphemism for someone who is drunk, often used in relation to public figures.

Tizzy
1. Gaudy. 2. To get yourself worked up about something.

Toe jam
The dirt under toenails or between the toes.

Toey
1. Anxious or bad-tempered. 2. Sexually hot to trot. *He's as toey as a Roman sandal.*

Tom tits
The shits. *He gives me the tom tits.*

Tonsil hockey
French or tongue kissing.

Too-hard basket
Metaphysical place for matters you don't want to address.

Toorak tractor
A flashy, four-wheel drive vehicle that rarely leaves the inner city. Named after the expensive inner-Melbourne suburb of Toorak. *Also* North Shore shopping trolley (in Sydney).

Tooshie
Upset. *Don't get tooshie with me.*

Top, tops
Excellent. *Simon is a top bloke. That's tops.*

Top drop
A good bottle of wine.

Ugly as a hatful of arseholes
By Australian standards, someone this ugly is probably a more frightening proposition than a person with a head like a robber's dog.

Top of the wozza
First class, excellent.

Touch of the toms
Got the shits. Rhyming slang for **tom tits**.

Trackie, trackie daks
Tracksuit, tracksuit pants.

Trolley dolly
A flight attendant or **hostie**.

Troppo
Mentally disturbed (as if affected by the sun in the tropics).

Trot
Might be a good or bad trot, when things are going well or not so well.

INITIALS #3
RBT *Random breath testing*
RDO *Rostered day off*
RTFM *Read the fucking manual*
SBD *Silent but deadly (fart)*
VPL *Visible panty line*
WHS *Wandering hands society, said by women of men*

Truckie
Truck or semi-trailer driver.

True blue, true blue Aussie
Genuine, loyal, authentically Australian.

Try-on, trying it on
An attempt to deceive someone or to get something without entitlement.

Tucker
Food.

Tuckerbag
A bag for storing food in the bush.

Turps
Cheap alcohol. *Also* on the turps and hitting the turps.

Twanger
A polite version of **wanker**.

Two bites of the cherry
Two opportunities to make a point or do something. (From **Aussie Rules** when players have a couple of attempts at a **mark**.)

Two bob each way
Sit on the fence, equivocate.

Two men and a dog
Not a very big crowd.

Two-pot screamer
A cheap drunk. From the small glass of beer known in some parts of Australia as a pot.

Tyre-kicker
A critical person who lacks expertise.

FAIR GO
This phrase is from the game of two-up and is the call from the ringie that all is ready for the toss. It is used, by some, to describe a trait of the quintessential Aussie, a desire for equality. Everyone deserves a fair go. Fair go is also used as an expression of exasperation or protest at an apparent lack of fairness. Come on ump, fair go.

U

Uee, uey
A U-turn, turn 360 degrees on a road. Also used metaphorically for a change of mind.

Um and ah
Be indecisive.

Ump, umpie, umpy
Umpire.

Unco
Short for uncoordinated.

Underdaks or undies
Underpants.

Underwhelmed
Not very pleased, excited or impressed about something.

Up his alley
Particularly suited to a person's likes or expertise. *That job is right up his alley.*

Up a gumtree
In trouble.

Up the duff
Pregnant.

Up there, Cazaly
An encouraging cheer, especially in regard to high marks in **Aussie Rules**.
After the legendary Australian Rules footballer Roy Cazaly.

Up yourself
Full of yourself, having a big ego.

Ute
A utility truck.

OCCUPATIONS (of a sort) #1
Ambo *Ambulance officer*
Blockie *Owner of a small block of land*
Boatie *Small boat owner*
Boardie *Surfboard rider*
Bushy, bushie *Someone who lives in the bush*
Chalkie *Teacher*
Clubbie *Surf club member*
Delo *Union delegate*
Firie, fire-ie, firee *Fireman*

V

Vatican roulette
The rhythm method of contraception.

Vegies
Vegetables.

Veg out
To do nothing.

Veranda over the toyshop, or toolshed
A euphemism for a big stomach on a man. *Also* Awning over the toyshop.

Vinnies
A St Vincent de Paul op shop.

Vote with your feet
Express your disapproval by walking away from something.

> **What a bunch of galahs**
> *This type of Australian parrot can be invoked to describe any display of particularly crass stupidity or counter-productive behaviour, or to lampoon important 'gala' events.*

W

WACA
Main cricket ground in Perth (West Australian Cricket Association).

Wag
To be absent without permission, particularly from school.

Wake up to yourself
Be more sensible, pull yourself together.

Walkabout
Originally nomadic wandering by Aboriginal people. Now generally used to suggest a loss of concentration.

Walkover
An easy win.

Walloper
A police officer.

Wanker
Person who carries on in a self-indulgent, egotistical, pretentious manner. General expression of derision. *Also* **twanger, owner operator**.

Washer-upperer
The person who washes the dishes.

Watering hole
A pub.

Wedding tackle
The male sexual organs.

Weekend warriors
Army reserve.

Weekender
Holiday house.

Weirdo
Someone who behaves eccentrically.

Well oiled
Drunk.

Who cut the dog in half?
This simple but startling question does not require the intervention of the RSPCA but is a polite Australian way of asking, 'Who farted?'

Westie
A person from the western suburbs of Sydney often viewed, unfairly, as uncultured.

Whacko
Exclamation of approval.

Wharfie
A waterside worker.

What a ripper!
That's fabulous.

What's the go?
What's happening?

What's your game?
What are you up to?

Whingeing Pom
A English person thought to be always criticising and complaining about life in Australia. Now used with a degree of affection.

White-ant
To destroy another's character or undermine them. *He's whiteanted me with the boss.*

Whitefella
A non-Aboriginal person of European descent.

White maggot
An **Aussie Rules** football umpire. Recently adapted to 'yellow maggot' because of a change of uniform colour.

White pointers
A woman sunbaking topless. Also, incidentally, a species of shark.

White-shoe brigade
Queensland property developers from the 1980s.

OCCUPATIONS (of a sort) #2
Journo *Journalist*
Linie *A telephone line worker*
Lowie *A lowlife*
Muso *Musician*
Pollie *Politician*
Pyro *Pyromaniac*
Sparkie *Electrician*
Subbie *Subcontractor*

Whole shebang
Everything, all of it.

Whoops-a-daisy
An exclamation of surprise.

Widow-maker
A dead branch on a tree, which may snap off and kill a person below.

Willy-willy
A dusty swirling wind.

Wing-nut
A person with protruding ears.

Winner
Something that is fabulous. *He's onto a winner.*

Who's up who and who's paying the rent?
The questioner here is not necessarily asking about other people's sex life but wants to know about the power and organisational relationships with which he/she is confronted.

Within cooee
Close enough.

Wog
A person of Mediterranean or Middle Eastern descent. Less derogatory than it once was but still potentially offensive.

Wog TV
Special Broadcasting Service (SBS) television, Australia's multicultural public broadcaster.

Wogball
Soccer.

Wogfood
Traditional food of Mediterranean or Middle Eastern people.

Woop woop
The middle of nowhere.

Woozy
Muddled, confused, drunk.

Work like a drover's dog
Work very hard.

Wormburner
A ball which keeps low in cricket or football, a grubber.

Worrywart
A person who constantly worries unnecessarily.

Wouldn't it
An expression of frustration, abbreviated from 'Wouldn't it root you?'

Wowser
A fun spoiler, puritan.

Wrinklie
An old person.

Write-off
1. Unable to do anything because of intoxication. 2. A car not worth repairing.

Wurring your slurds
Spoonerism for slurring your words (when drunk).

WALTZING MATILDA
Considered the unofficial national anthem (the official anthem being Advance Australia Fair) and often sung at sporting events.

XYZ

Yabber
Talk a lot.

Yabbie
Freshwater crayfish.

Yack, yak
Talk or chatter.

Yacker, yakka
Manual labour or work.

Yahoo
A loudmouthed, loutish person.

Yankeeland
United States. (Used recently by Prime Minister John Howard.)

Yarn
A conversation, usually involving an anecdote.

Yartz
Strine pronunciation of 'the arts'.

Yawn
A bore.

Yeah, no
A recent addition to the language. Does it mean yes or no? It may mean either—listen to what comes next.

Yob, yobbo
A slob, hooligan, lout.

Yonks
A long time. *He's been gone for yonks.*

Yonnie
A stone or pebble, good for throwing (Victoria).

You game?
Are you brave enough to do something.

You little ripper
That's fantastic.

You wouldn't read about it
Something completely unexpected or unimaginable.

You're a dag
You're funny, usually said affectionately.

You're not Robinson Crusoe
You're not alone, you're not the only one with a problem.

Wouldn't touch that with a forty-foot pole.
Even after over thirty years' familiarity with the metric system, the mythical forty-foot pole remains the ultimate Australian measure of aversion.

You're not wrong
You're right.

You're right
You're welcome. That's okay.

Youse
Plural form of you. In 1986, after winning a world boxing title fight, Jeff Fenech said, 'I love youse all'. Not the first use of youse but a memorable one.

You've got to be in it to win it
You have to have a go, or get involved. Originally used in relation to a lottery or raffle.

Yuck, yucko, yucky
Exclamation of disgust.

> **Wouldn't be dead for quids**
> *An inverted way of saying that life is really pretty good and that things are going very well. In Aussie slang, the quid is still legal tender.* See also **Not quite the full quid.**

Yum, yummo, yummy
Tasty.

Yummy mummies
Attractive, well-dressed, young mothers. Often spotted dropping their children off at school, usually in a four-wheel drive vehicle.

Z-grade
The worst quality.

Zizz
A nap.

Zorba
Affectionate nickname for a person of Greek ancestry.

SEE YOU LATER

Madame Chen, a visitor from China, said her farewells to a family she'd become friendly with. 'See you later', the family replied. Madame Chen waited patiently, not aware that her Aussie friends had said their goodbyes.

STOP THE PRESS

Some colourful last-minute additions.

As busy as a brickie in Beirut
No longer appropriate to Beirut but could be adapted to Baghdad.

On every board but the breadboard
A description of someone who is a director on numerous corporate boards.

Would take a fly from a blind spider
A description of a mean and nasty person.

He shops around the corner
A euphemistic description of a homosexual.

Would go to the opening of an envelope (or a wound)
The propensity of a socialite to attend all the social functions to which he or she is invited.

Tell 'im he's dreamin'
Michael Caton's character in the movie, *The Castle*, made this comment about the optimism of people's advertised prices in the *Trading Post*, a publication full of ads for second-hand items.

The politics of the warm inner glow
The right-wing faction of the Australian Labor Party views some of the policies of the left wing as heartwarming but unrealistic.